Dangerous Women

Bringing back what "Act Like A Lady" looks like as we raise the bar of morals, decency and integrity throughout our country.

By Eileen Marx

This is a book of values, of principles, a code of conduct for women to walk in and live out for today and future generations. Taking God's word to heart, applying His principles and living out what it truly looks like to be a woman created in the image of God.

To all the Dangerous Mothers, Daughters, Sisters, Aunties and Wives living in the 21st Century.

You are each here for such a time as this. Your generation is in desperate need for you to proclaim God's goodness, purpose and love.

In His Love,

♥

Eileen

Table of Contents

What makes a woman dangerous? 5

Compassion, Conviction and Commitment 6
    Compassion 6
    Conviction 7
    Commitment 8

Eight Codes of Conduct and Values for Dangerous Women 11
    CODE I: She Takes Her Rightful Place 12
    CODE II: She Walks In Her Identity, Inheritance and Value 22
    CODE III: She Understands the Difference Between Who She Is and What She Does 29
    CODE IV: She Lives Out Her Powerful Influence ... 39
    CODE V: She Understands How Her Words and Actions Represent Herself 45
    CODE VI: She Takes Risks 52
    CODE VII: She Doesn't Look For the Lazy or Easy Way, Nor Does She Make Excuses 56
    CODE VIII: She Values Character & Reputation Over Status Quo 63

What makes a woman dangerous?

A dangerous woman knows who she is and her intrinsic worth and value in this life. She knows her greatest assets are prayer and forgiveness. She lives this out by staying close to God and seeking His heart and mind for those in her life. She does not trust in her own understanding, but rather she trusts in the Lord to lead and direct her steps.

She trusts in the Lord with all her heart and does not lean on her own understanding, but in all her ways she acknowledges Him. (Proverbs 3:5)

Her greatest strength is her wisdom, which is rooted in the fear of the Lord. This is true for every race, culture and nation.

A Dangerous Woman lives by the Three C's:

Compassion, Conviction and Commitment

Compassion

> *When He saw the multitudes, He was moved with compassion for them, because they were weary and scattered, like sheep having no shepherd.* — Matthew 9:36

The harvest truly is plentiful, but the laborers are few.

Following her Savior's example, this woman sees the needs of others and doesn't wait for others to act. She possesses awareness, acknowledging those needs, and steps up to provide what she can when it is in her power and ability to do so.

Jesus moved with His Father's love and gave of Himself to the hurting and broken. Seeing the pain and harassment from the enemy, He healed and freed many from the grip of the wicked one.

In the same way, a dangerous woman is filled with the love of the Father and freely gives of herself. She sees the needs of those around her and is moved with compassion.

Wanting to imitate and follow her Lord and Savior, a dangerous woman does not rely on the whims of her emotions or the pull of the culture. She trusts her life to Jesus and relies on Him for the outcome.

> *I am the Vine, you are the branches, he who abides in Me, and I in him, bears much fruit. For without Me, you can do nothing.* — John 15:5

Conviction

For a dangerous woman, choosing to walk in her convictions is a daily choice.

> *Choose for yourselves today whom you will serve…* — Joshua 24:15

She walks in this confidence and promise.

> *For where two or three are gathered together in My name, I am there in the midst of them.* — Matthew 18:20

There are many worldly things beckoning for her attention, pulling at her from all directions. She stays settled, focused and filled with a heart of purpose to follow Jesus at whatever the cost. She is guided by truth and is keen to detect lies and deception.

> *My sheep hear My voice, and I know them, and they follow Me.* — John 10:27

Commitment

She prioritizes her life to fit with her commitments: faith, family and her God-given domain. She understands commitment and what that may cost her. She is reliable and consistent. Her "yes" means "yes," and her "no" means "no."

> *But let your 'Yes' be 'Yes,' and your 'No,' be 'No.' For whatever is more than these is from the evil one.* — Matthew 5:37

They recognized the need to get back to the basics in God's two greatest commandments given to Moses on Mount Sinai. Jesus reinforced these commandments in the Gospels.

The first:

> *You shall love the LORD your God with all your heart, with all your soul, and with all your mind.*
> — Matthew 22:37

And the second:

> *You shall love your neighbor as yourself. — Matthew 22:39*
>
> *She opens her mouth with wisdom and on her tongue is the law of kindness. — Proverbs 31:26*

If dangerous women took this to heart, we could see a change in the tide of our own country. We would most certainly witness Americans turn from their bitterness, anger, resentfulness and desire for revenge to a place of grace, compassion, forgiveness and love. Imagine the lives that could be affected, their abundance multiplied by this simple act.

> *And above all things, have fervent love for one another, for 'love will cover a multitude of sins.'*
> — 1 Peter 4:8

The basic need of every soul on the planet is to know they are loved and valued. The enemy of our soul capitalizes on this and, with ease, convinces people that they are not loved and are not of any value or worth. This drives people to prove to themselves and others that they are valuable by using the world's standards as a gauge, leading them to engage in high-risk, degrading behavior and compromised values. This often desperate behavior may result in damage to reputation, character and even a loss of life.

Eight Codes of Conduct and Values for Dangerous Women

CODE i: She Takes Her Rightful Place.

CODE ii: She Walks In Her Identity, Inheritance and Value.

CODE iii: She Understands the Difference Between Who She Is and What She Does.

CODE iv: She Lives Out Her Powerful Influence.

CODE v: She Understands How Her Words and Actions Represent Herself.

CODE vi: She Takes Risks.

CODE vii: She Doesn't Look For the Lazy or Easy Way, Nor Does She Make Excuses.

CODE viii: She Values Character & Reputation Over Status Quo.

CODE 1: **She Takes Her Rightful Place.**

Dangerous women take their rightful place in the Lord Jesus Christ, who is seated at the right hand of God Almighty.

> *…And what is the exceeding greatness of His power towards us who believe, according to the working of His mighty power which He worked in Christ when He raised Him from the dead and seated Him at His right hand in the heavenly places.* — Ephesians 1:19-20

> *…and raised us up together and made us sit together in the heavenly places in Christ Jesus.* — Ephesians 2:6

This woman who sees Jesus as her Lord and Savior puts Him in His rightful place in her life and then takes her rightful place with Him in the heavenlies. He is first before everything else.

First thing in the morning, He is on her mind. She is eager to spend time with Him, converse with Him, hear His voice and read His word. This woman understands this relationship is the secret to every other relationship on the planet. She fully grasps the strength, wisdom and courage that is needed each day to follow Him and be His hands and feet to a broken world. Love and devotion are what moves her, not religion, legalism or duty. She knows Him, trusts Him and believes He is with her always.

> *So confident had his faith become through the years of asking and receiving, so intimate was his communion with God from uncounted hours spent in audience with Him, that his whole countenance and his whole being manifested the dignity of a member of the royal household of heaven.* — George Mueller

Her understanding of her position in the family of God is equally important. As a member of the household of heaven, there are untold treasures to be found here on Earth as we wait for our eternal promotion.

> *That the God of our Lord Jesus Christ, the father of glory, may give to you the spirit of wisdom and revelation in the knowledge of Him, the eyes of your understanding being enlightened, that you may know what is the hope of His calling, what are the riches of the glory of His inheritance in the saints, and what is the exceeding greatness of His power towards us who*

believe, according to the working of His mighty power. — Ephesians 1:17-19

Having material possessions pales in comparison to the strength, wisdom and courage that comes from spending time in the presence of God our Creator, the Holy Spirit, and the sweet fellowship with Jesus. This cannot be purchased or counterfeited. The fruit of this discipline brings confidence and courage in the lives of those who invest in Him.

What is the benefit of this relationship?

When the world is out of control, when government leaders lie and hide the truth and news media outlets are complicit in perpetuating these lies, when the wealthy abuse their power to control the masses and push their ungodly agenda, and we watch our loved ones forced to choose between a paycheck or their principles, when the world shakes in fear, driven by its own uncertainty and anger, we can rest in the fact that God is in control and always will be. He is the one who will work all things for good for those who love Him and are called according to His purposes.

We no longer need to lose our temper, raising our blood pressure trying to figure out how to expose those who promote evil behind the scenes. We stay close to Him in conversation, meditation and we wait on Him. We listen for His voice to give us our marching orders. We remain confident in Him. We don't let evil rule, and we don't sit back and wait for others to act. We take back what is ours, knowing and believing we are on the winning side as we stay near Him; we move with victory.

It's time to take what belongs to us: the God-given rights that have been bestowed upon our loved ones and ourselves. It begins with the most important relationship this side of eternity.

What does an earthly relationship look like with our Heavenly Father?

Can you think of someone in your life whom you can't wait to spend time with, to hear his voice, to see her face, to hear how their day went, to be able to share the details of your own day?

This is exactly how it feels when you spend that time with Jesus. You can't wait to talk with Him, tell Him all about your day, the mishaps, the aggravations, the funny events, the embarrassing moments and even the frustrating things that you struggle to see past. You know if you can just sit with Him for a little bit, you'll start seeing things differently. You genuinely look forward to having those moments together.

He helps to ground you and encourage you and even point out your blind spots. He is so very present; He loves to hear your voice confiding in Him. He's like a parent who is able to see everything his child does but still loves to hear the child tell the story. Even if it's just a moment together, He treasures it, and then like a parent watching that child skip away, He must smile and hold His heart.

VALUE OF HER AUTHORITY

To be like a child, yet feel like a dangerous woman, may seem like an oxymoron, but I believe it is a key ingredient to living in such freedom with simplicity and power.

This woman understands clearly that all forces of darkness, powers and principalities are under the authority of Jesus Christ.

> *Far above all principality and power and might and dominion, and every name that is named not only in this age but also in that which is to come.*
> *— Ephesians 1:21*

As she walks in obedience with Him, she walks in His authority, destroying the chaos, exposing evil, exposing the lies, and all those things that run contrary to the mind and will of God. In His authority she brings order into her life and into the lives of those who God brings to her.

Since ancient times, warfare has been won by those who took the high ground. When you can position yourself in higher ground you can see your enemy more clearly. As believers, we've been given this perspective. Let's take full advantage of it.

This woman does not fear death, nor does she count her life more valuable than anyone else's. She knows her days on this earth are already planned out and counted, so she walks with confidence and determination.

She is not gullible, naive, or easily swayed by persuasive words or those who have the gift of manipulation. Because she spends time with her God, she recognizes the counterfeit voices and messages of false teachings and the false narratives of the day. She fears God and takes to heart the understanding that fear of man is a snare, but fear of the Lord is the beginning of understanding.

VALUE OF CONFIDENCE

Confidence is her calling card and determination is her fuel. She believes every day counts.

> *There is no neutral ground in the Universe. Every square inch and every split second are claimed by God, and counterclaimed by Satan.* — C.S Lewis

Understanding this truth, so eloquently stated by C.S. Lewis, gives a dangerous woman proper perspective. She identifies the importance of each decision she makes for herself, as well as her family.

VALUE OF PRAYER

She also recognizes the utmost importance of prayer and surrounding herself with prayer warriors for her mission. Prayer is the most powerful weapon available to every human on the planet.

HOW DOES THIS CODE SPEAK TO ME?

WHAT DO I WANT TO CHANGE TO LIVE OUT THIS CODE BETTER?

𝕮𝕺𝕯𝕰 ii: She Walks In Her Identity, Inheritance and Value.

A dangerous woman understands her identity, inheritance and intrinsic worth. As she walks in her identity, she is not pulled into futile arguments or endless word battles with ignorant people. In conversations, she is tempered, respectful, thoughtful and engaging. She knows who she is and doesn't have to prove her intelligence — let alone herself.

VALUE OF SELF IMPROVEMENT

<u>She studies</u> for the sake of her own self-improvement. She is well read in topics that are important and is a constant student of what is righteous and true. As a humble learner, she knows there is much more knowledge for her to gain. She seeks qualified leaders and teachers who also have a strong understanding of who they are. A dangerous woman understands the value of time and seeks to use her time wisely.

VALUE OF RECOGNIZING TOXIC EMOTIONS

<u>Recognizing toxic emotions</u> allows her to deal with them promptly as she knows these feelings can affect her soul, leading her down a slippery path of anger,

resentment, bitterness, jealousy, pride, pity and more. Toxic emotions can compromise her God-given mission and lead her away from the sense of peace she has with her Lord and Savior. Forgiveness is her constant go-to and compassion is the garment she wears as she recognizes that all people are broken and in need of a Savior.

Insecurities are tied to the lies from the enemy of her soul. She knows she must capture these lies and bring them to the footstool of Jesus. She doesn't negotiate with these lies or nurse them, she is quick to recognize them and assert her God-given authority over them. She understands the power of the blood of Jesus and proclaims it over her mind when she is being assaulted with lies and negative thoughts.

VALUE OF BRINGING VALUE

A dangerous woman lives out her <u>value by bringing value to others</u>. She sees herself as a direct conduit of Jesus' own hands and feet as she goes where He directs her. She can see the value of so many who have been abused, abandoned, taken advantage of and become outcasts of society. She takes the scripture to heart when Jesus says:

And the King will answer and say to them, 'Assuredly I say to you, Inasmuch as you did it to one of the least of these, My brethren you did it to Me.' — Matthew 25:40

She understands the value of every person is not measured by their level of education, their bank account, the car they drive, their clothing, homes, jets or jewels, but each individual is measured at the Cross — the most powerful equalizer of all. Our value is the same at the foot of the Cross.

Whether her platform is the classroom, kitchen, doctor's office, boardroom or stage, she is ready to give her all to the task at hand. No task is beneath her, nor a challenge too far above her. She looks at the roles she's given as an opportunity to speak truth and live out that truth. She uses these roles to grow and bring life to others. When a soul knows they are loved by the Father, that He sees them, that they are special to Him, it settles them.

Her inheritance is that with the saints, and she understands she is an heir to a magnificent inheritance.

> *... giving thanks to the Father who has qualified us to be partakers of the inheritance of the saints of the light. — Col 1:12*

It is the Father who qualifies us, not our own works.

Looking forward to an inheritance provides healthy motivation for a dangerous woman in her day-to-day life.

HOW DOES THIS CODE SPEAK TO ME?

WHAT DO I WANT TO CHANGE TO LIVE OUT THIS CODE BETTER?

CODE iii: She Understands the Difference Between Who She Is and What She Does.

A dangerous woman appreciates and understands the difference between who she is and what she does. Each of these are distinct attributes and not meant to be confused.

She understands that, regardless of her accomplishments, she isn't any more or less valuable to God. What she DOES is a vocation, a skill, a hobby, and that changes throughout her lifetime. Who she IS does not change as she is of great value and worth, created in the image of God Almighty.

Whether married or single, she recognizes her value in this world. She doesn't have the need to compete with men nor prove her worth. She is fully aware of who she is, but more importantly, to Whom she belongs.

VALUE OF BEING SECOND

She can willingly come alongside her husband or co-worker and see how her strengths, gifts and calling can be used to help make their lives better. She is encouraging, challenging, and ready to step into a leadership role or a support role depending on what is needed at the time. She doesn't feel threatened if a man is stronger or more capable in certain areas, as she knows that she, too, has different strengths and capabilities than a man.

She doesn't feel threatened by other women as she recognizes that each of us has our own set of strengths and weaknesses. She understands that we are all running our own races, each of us in different lanes, all trying to do our best. In the end, a dangerous woman's goal is to be useful and disciplined in ways that bring those around her a higher quality of life and dignity.

Deborah, a prophetess from the book of Judges, is a great example of how a dangerous woman steps into her place. A dangerous woman not only comes in the flow of God's Word, but she, herself, speaks God's Word. And that's what we see Deborah doing throughout this story. Calling Barak to battle against Sisera, Deborah says:

> *Has not the Lord, the God of Israel, commanded you?* — Judges 4:6

Deborah's mouth overflows with God's Word in commands (Judges 4:6, 14), judgments (Judges 4:9) and promises (Judges 4:7, 14).

Deborah's strength comes from God's Word. When we celebrate the strength of Deborah, we also celebrate her obedience to God in spite of what the outcome would be. The Word of God is on the tongue of today's strong women as they often were in both the Old and New Testaments.

Deborah clearly respects and embraces Barak's God-ordained role. Even when Barak is afraid to obey, Deborah does not belittle or replace him — instead, she helps him. She immediately agrees to go with him as he asks. Now, she does give God's judgment on Barak's weakness. Sisera, himself, will die, not by Barak's hand, but by the hand of another strong woman named Jael.

Her story is also in the Old Testament Book of Judges and tells how Sisera, a commander in the Canaanite army, flees a disastrous battle with the Israelites. He is offered milk and shelter by Jael, a married woman of the Kenite tribe. When Sisera falls asleep, Jael drives a tent peg through his skull. These two strong women bookend the narrative like pillars holding up the house.

VALUE OF CONFIDENCE AND RESPECT

<u>Confidence and respect</u> are key!

A single woman is not desperate to find a man — certainly not just any man. She holds fast in seeking a man with the qualities that will match her own heart and endure a lifetime. A viable contender who can match a dangerous woman's heart is a man who loves God, honors and respects people, values life and sees his own life as an extension of his faith.

She doesn't fret but prays for him and herself and the right timing.

VALUE OF KEEPING HERSELF FOR FUTURE HUSBAND

She keeps herself for her future husband as she understands this is a valuable and sacred gift, believing that God has the right man in mind for her. Even if she has made wrong choices in the past, she presses forward and doesn't live in that past but looks forward to all that God has for her.

VALUE OF BEING A WIFE

As a married woman, she takes her role as a wife seriously; she is committed to the covenant she made with her husband and her God. Her incredible strength comes from understanding the purpose of marriage, as she believes the wisdom that was spoken thousands of years ago is still relevant today.

> *And He answered and said to them, 'Have you not read that He who made them at the beginning made them male and female,' and said, 'For this reason a man shall leave his father and mother and be joined to his wife and the two shall become one flesh?'* — Matthew 19:4-5

This relationship was crafted meticulously from the very beginning. Being joined as "one flesh" is a great mystery as it is much more than just the physical aspect.

VALUE OF HER INFLUENCE

A dangerous <u>woman's influence</u> in her husband's life is also his greatest asset. Because she is trustworthy, he confides in her and has no fear she may betray his confidence. Her advice and wisdom are something he treasures and considers essential to his life.

> *The heart of her husband safely trusts her; so, he will have no lack of gain. She does him good not evil all the days of her life.* — Proverbs 31:11

> *He is confident of her love, care, and fidelity. He dares trust her with his soul secrets and he does not doubt her faith, love, and care of his family.* — Trapp

She not only sees her role as a support role alongside her husband, but she also embraces this, planning and preparing diligently in order to create a safe haven and a place of rest and peace. She brings gain to her husband on many levels and in great measure.

> *I am the emotional caretaker of my husband. Because I care for him in the home, he can care for a nation* — Nancy Reagan

Like any military operation, there is a commanding general who is responsible for the outcome of the mission but relies heavily on his blueprints and support team to see it come to fruition. If his men do not follow his lead, the outcome may be devastating.

Likewise, the God-loving husband relies on his wife — his support team — along with her faith and her proven character. He needs her to come alongside him and not only view the blueprints to the mission of their marriage and family, but also to provide insight and wisdom to help establish a plan.

Physical intimacy is reserved for marriage between a man and woman. Intimacy is a very important aspect of the relationship between husband and wife. This woman understands the strength this oneness brings to the marriage on a regular basis and, at times, the healing it provides during periods of stress and the unexpected. During stressful and challenging times, there is much healing and repairing that can be done through this beautiful act if both are willing to surrender their toxic emotions, forgiving and receiving forgiveness in the process.

Husband and wife: one made from the elements of dirt, the other taken from a rib — a lifelong journey of the physical, mental, emotional and spiritual — together as one.

HOW DOES THIS CODE SPEAK TO ME?

WHAT DO I WANT TO CHANGE TO LIVE OUT THIS CODE BETTER?

CODE iv: She Lives Out Her Powerful Influence.

Dangerous women know the powerful influence they wield in their world.

> *The Hand That Rocks the Cradle Is the Hand That Rules The World.* — William Ross Wallace.

This was first published in 1865 under the title, "What Rules the World?"

Women, particularly mothers, have a decisive influence on the future direction of society because they raise and nurture the next generation. Motherhood is one of the most sacred offices in humankind. The whole aspect, from being able to conceive to growing life, giving birth to nurturing another life, motherhood is truly magnificent. This process does not stop once the baby is born. The responsibilities continue and become greater as the child grows. The mother who understands this role continues to give life by teaching and instructing the values and God-given mandates to live by. Motherhood is a full-time, full-sized job if done right. The job description is endless, and the accolades are very few and far between.

The task of motherhood rarely feels rewarding and is often mocked as a "trivial, meaningless job" — even considered lazy by those who don't understand this high calling and would rather belittle it than acknowledge its importance and honor. Nonetheless, a dangerous woman knows the lifelong value she is providing to her children as she sacrifices much to put in the time and effort to raise them.

Look at Sparta culture.

Sparta was a warrior society in ancient Greece that reached its height of power after defeating rival city-state Athens in the Peloponnesian War (431-404 BC).

Spartan women were educated, had a reputation for being independent-minded, and enjoyed more status and freedom than the other Greek women. While they played no role in the military, female Spartans often received a formal education.

According to ancient Spartan ideology, the primary role of adult women was to bear and raise healthy children. This focus on childbearing likely attributed to the emphasis on physical fitness in Spartan women, as it was believed that physically stronger women would have healthier children.

A dangerous woman's husband is also a strong and wise man who understands his wife's strength and the sacrifices she makes for her children.

Hear, my son, your father's instruction, and forsake not your mother's teaching, for they are a graceful garland for your head and pendants for your neck. — Proverbs 1:8-9

Her children rise up and call her blessed; her husband also, and he praises her: 'Many women have done excellently, but you surpass them all.' — Proverbs 31:28-31

Every one of you shall revere his mother and his father. — Leviticus 19:3

I have no greater joy than to hear that my children are walking in the truth. — 3 John 1:4

VALUE OF BEING KIND

As a woman in this world, she sees <u>the powerful impact she can have on others by simply being kind</u>, preferring to tend to others' needs before her own, often while lending encouraging words.

It is more blessed to give than to receive. — Acts 20:35

HOW DOES THIS CODE SPEAK TO ME?

WHAT DO I WANT TO CHANGE TO LIVE OUT THIS CODE BETTER?

𝔒𝔒𝔇𝔈 𝔳: She Understands How Her Words and Actions Represent Herself.

When given a platform to speak, a dangerous woman comes well-prepared and respectful of her audience. She prepares and educates herself about her topic and her audience, so her words will be relevant and meaningful. She's not trying to win a popularity contest, but rather she recognizes the opportunity to speak truth and direct people to thoughtful, righteous and worthy values.

VALUE OF WHAT SHE MEDTIATES ON

She understands that how and what she meditates on affects how she sees herself and those around her. She doesn't allow her mind to drift off to mindless thinking or the empty philosophies of lost people who try to lead people down a path of destruction. Very aware of the false teachings and false narratives of the day, she is highly selective about who she listens to and what is allowed in her home.

> *For of this sort are those who creep into households and make captives of gullible women loaded down with sins, led away by various lusts, always*

learning and never able to come to the knowledge of the truth. — *2 Timothy 3:6-7*

VALUE OF UNDERSTANDING THE POWER OF HER FEMINITY

Dangerous women understand <u>the power of their femininity</u> and do not get pulled into the lies that revealing our feminine aspects brings us more value. In fact, just the opposite is true. Exposing our assets to the world reveals our insecurities within by demonstrating the need for attention and affirmation from others. Preserving this aspect of our femininity for our husbands reveals true confidence and self-worth, a value that he will respect, honor and protect.

A dangerous gentleman worthy of her sees her modesty as a powerful asset and a quality greatly admired. He, too, will guard and protect her honor.

> *Man looks at the outward appearance, but the Lord looks at the heart.* — 1 Samuel 16:7

She understands that just because women are referred to as "the weaker vessel" (1 Peter 3:7), it does not mean they are to be taken advantage of or that they have no right to defend themselves or their loved ones. She looks at this as her "God-given right" and takes it seriously. With this, she trains her mind and body to be prepared for such an event.

In fact, the mental aspect of self-defense is just as important as physical skill, even when it comes to the use of weapons.

She incorporates the 4 "A's" into her everyday life:

Awareness: Always aware of her surroundings, using all of her senses: sight, smell, sound and unseen discernment that warns her of potential problems, including awareness of suspicious activity and nefarious characters.

Assessment: Evaluates a situation and mentally prepares for execution of next steps, if needed.

Avoidance: Whenever possible, she allows herself an opportunity to avoid and escape potentially harmful situations.

Action: If required, she steps into action to thwart the threat and secure herself and others from harm and injury.

She doesn't let fear overtake her emotions, avoiding the "what ifs." Instead, she trusts in God and prepares herself through practice and training.

Her understanding of the Second Amendment to the U.S. Constitution is strong and secure, and she can confidentially recite the famous quote:

Molon Labe (Mow Lawn Lah Bay) — A Greek phrase meaning, "Come and take [them]," attributed to King Leonidas of Sparta as a defiant response to the demand that his soldiers lay down their weapons.

HOW DOES THIS CODE SPEAK TO ME?

WHAT DO I WANT TO CHANGE TO LIVE OUT THIS CODE BETTER?

CODE vi: She Takes Risks.

Dangerous women take risks at the cost of their own reputation for the sake of what's right, even when it doesn't fit the modern-day narrative. She is not concerned or impressed by the bandwagon mentality, but instead, she recognizes what is true and righteous in God's sight.

> *She extends her hands to the poor; Yes, she reaches out her hand to the needy.* — Proverbs 31:20

> *Assuredly, I say to you, inasmuch as you did it to one of the least of these, My brethren, you did it to Me.* — Matthew 25:40

At times this may require the use of self-defense weapons to protect innocent ones or those who cannot protect themselves. She doesn't see her own life as more valuable than others. She understands her character is more valuable than her reputation. In the end, she is not moved by the opinion of others, but rather she lives to hear these six words at the end of her life on Earth and at the beginning of her new life in heaven.

> *Well done thy good and faithful servant...* — Matthew 25:23

HOW DOES THIS CODE SPEAK TO ME?

WHAT DO I WANT TO CHANGE TO LIVE OUT THIS CODE BETTER?

CODE vii: She Doesn't Look For the Lazy or Easy Way, Nor Does She Make Excuses.

A dangerous woman does not look for the easy way out of difficult situations. She presses into her daily life and the challenges that are presented with purpose and conviction. She is not easily offended as she keeps her mind on Christ and relies on His grace to help her in life's situations.

> *He who is slothful in his work is a brother to him who is a great destroyer. — Proverbs 18:9*

VALUE OF TAKING RESPONSIBILITY

Taking full responsibility for her mental, physical, emotional and spiritual health is another dangerous woman's character trait.

She knows she is the only one who can do this. She sees each aspect of her life as a stewardship opportunity.

She is fully aware of how each one of these is interlinked with one another. She must not allow her mind to feed on a diet of ungodly ideas through music, movies, and podcasts or other entertainment. Ideas that are contrary to God's design include: relativism (the doctrine that knowledge, truth and morality exists in relation to culture, society or historical context and are not absolute) and humanism (the theory that focuses on human beings rather than supernatural or divine insight, that stresses that human beings are inherently good, and that basic needs are vital to human behaviors).

Another pitfall belief is the idea that, "I must take care of number one."

She knows these will pull her away from a holy mindset that is critical for her health and walk with the Lord. She also understands that hanging out with people who do not have the same mindset is equally dangerous, bearing in mind this verse:

Bad company corrupts good morals. — 1 Corinthians 15:33

Taking care of her body through healthy eating and exercise are two non-negotiable commitments. She sees that the food she eats plays a huge part in how she feels. This is a discipline that she incorporates into her everyday life. She looks at her food preparation and planning with purpose, providing nourishing meals for herself and her loved ones. She knows that if she fails to plan in this area, she plans to fail. Nutrition is not an afterthought, but rather, a forethought. Eating fast food and convenience food as a normal diet actually takes life out of us. We must consider the fact that most of the ingredients found in them are not healthy foods at all but factory-created substances with added chemicals and fillers.

Eating once-living food is the best choice for our body as we have a built-in decoder that knows how to read the codes in these foods and utilize them for daily health, growth and repair of the body. Recognizing how wonderfully and fearfully our bodies are made motivates us to take care of ourselves.

> *I will praise You for I am fearfully and wonderfully made.* — Psalm 139:14

Exercise is another discipline that characterizes this woman, as it is an essential aspect that affects her whole being. Like quality food and nutrition, she incorporates exercise into her life and plans for it. Energy, mental focus, health and positive outlook are all benefits that come from exercise. How she feels about herself isn't about vanity, but instead, she has a desire to be her best and have energy to do those things in life she loves to do.

She girds herself with strength and strengthens her arms. — Proverbs 31:17

Our bodies have over 600 muscles and 200 bones all designed to move! Every system in our bodies benefits from movement. Our cardiovascular, nervous, musculoskeletal, endocrine, immune, respiratory, skin and digestive systems — as well as our psychological health — are all impacted directly by exercise.

She does not make excuses or blame others for her behavior and choices. She is gracious, humble and accepts the consequences of her actions. She owns up to the choices she makes and learns from them.

Blaming others and not taking responsibility are a sign of immaturity and an indication that she needs to grow in this area. Understanding that we all have areas we can grow in, she doesn't look at this as a failure but as an opportunity for growth. Likewise, she extends the same grace to others as they, too, have an opportunity to learn and grow as a result of their decisions, both good and bad.

HOW DOES THIS CODE SPEAK TO ME?

WHAT DO I WANT TO CHANGE TO LIVE OUT THIS CODE BETTER?

CODE viii: **She Values Character & Reputation Over Status Quo.**

Dangerous women who choose to take a stand on righteousness do not hesitate to do so for fear of backlash from those who disagree with their stance. They assess the cost, move with conviction and speak deliberately, knowing every word counts. They are bold and confident in their delivery and do not back down when met with hate speech, resistance and character assaults.

They can see the real entity behind these angry assaults and false accusations. They know how to defeat this entity and dismantle its tactics through battling in prayer. Prayer is truly the greatest asset and tool for this kind of battle.

She also understands the simple power of her sincere smile, encouraging words or a simple hug. These life-giving attributes are glaringly missing and dearly needed in today's world. Each one of these can bring a sense of value to an overwhelmed soul who's feeling worthless, inadequate and possibly ready to give up.

> *She openeth her mouth with wisdom; and in her tongue is the law of kindness.* — *Proverbs 31:26*

VALUE OF NOT FOLLOWING STATUS QUO

These women do not follow the status quo, they lead by example. Oftentimes, they are misunderstood because of their strong convictions. Their lives are marked by standing up for what's right, speaking out for what's wrong and calling evil what it is — EVIL— even when it's not popular. Although those who prefer the status quo do not like a dangerous woman's message, the truth speaks for itself.

With the ongoing deterioration in moral beliefs and convictions in this world, there has never been a greater time than now for women, real women, to step up, step out and be dangerous. Our nation is in a rapid decline in every area of influence: the family, the church, media, education, medicine, military and government.

There is an even greater need for men to stand up and take their place, as the responsibilities of a society falls on their shoulders.

> *Husbands, love your wives, just as Christ also loved the church and gave Himself for it.* — Ephesians 5:25

There are no more important roles for a man than the roles of husband and father. As men seek to righteously fulfill these roles, they become more like their Father in Heaven. Imagine how our world would be if every husband and father took this role to heart.

When men stand up and claim their authority and rightful place, women can let go of the reins and the desperate position they find themselves in. Especially in the home. Together, men and women can partner together to change the chaos and bring order into the home and community around them. We no longer need to change and control the chaos that is happening all around us.

Powerful shifts happen when women start respecting the men in their lives and stop making excuses for them. Allowing men to be men and challenging them to reject passivity and mediocrity in their lives gives them the encouragement to rise to their God-given roles. Physical suffering and enduring pain for causes greater than themselves doesn't hurt them, but makes them stronger.

VALUE OF RAISING YOUNG MEN

These women raising young men understand the <u>value of teaching boys at a young age who they are</u> and what incredible leaders they were made to be. Giving these young men an idea about the responsibilities they will have as leaders of their own families one day will provide an essential foundation. Strong mothers do not make excuses for their sons or keep them from pain (consequences from their actions), but hold them accountable for their actions and allow the consequences to do their job. It's also essential that a mother expects and demands respectful behavior from them.

Something incredible happens when men and women take their rightful places in the home and community. By embracing their proper positions and valuing the influence they possess, both men and women can work together to reach their mutual common goals.

Dangerous men and women don't get pulled into the emotional side of highly divisive issues and the extreme behavior that affects the masses. Instead, they are able to keep their wits about them and inject truth and reason when the opportunity arises. By courageously using their God-given platform to speak truth, they do their part in moving the needle back toward a God-honoring society.

Openly and defiantly we, as a nation, have pushed God out of all the great blessings and privileges He has bestowed upon us.

From the breakdown and distortion of family values to the perversion of what constitutes marriage — the very first institution that was created by God — our country has lost its way.

We are witnessing a breakdown of one our nation's greatest institution's, The Church, resulting in an almost unrecognizable, politically correct organization that has warmed itself to the culture, resulting in a loss of the Godly influence it was created to provide, to government leadership that has made a mockery of this once blessed nation through prideful and arrogant leaders with selfish ambition.
From allowing babies to be aborted to misleading millions of children through destructive school curriculum, we are seeing a country in moral decline.

From what was once recognized as the most powerful military in the world to a force that is now considered a fettered joke by our adversaries, America needs a reset.

I don't think it's too late to repent. We must turn back to Him, honor Him and ask for His forgiveness to cleanse us so that He may pour out His blessings on our great nation once again.

If My people who are called by My name will humble themselves and pray and seek My face and turn from their wicked ways, I will hear from heaven and will forgive their sins and heal their land. — 2 Chronicles 7:14

Let's make every day we have here count for something bigger than ourselves. Let's get off the treadmill that leads to the same thing over and over again. Let's get on the tractor and start plowing, taking back the ground that we have given over to the forces of darkness.

Women, can you hear the clarion call? Are you ready to be a dangerous woman for the sake of our children, families and future generations?

No resume is needed; no drawn-out plan is required. We just need a willing heart, disciplined mind and a spirit of sacrifice to take back what is rightfully ours. Let us be known as women of wisdom, kindness, character, conviction and compassion as we commit our today to a greater cause than ourselves and leave a worthwhile legacy for tomorrow.

A dangerous woman's loyalty and faith is to God, her Savior, her Prince of Peace. He is our purpose, our passion and our everything. We adjust to His plans and step with Him. We obey, we submit and we serve.

"For in Him we live and move and have our being..." — Acts 17:28

HOW DOES THIS CODE SPEAK TO ME?

WHAT DO I WANT TO CHANGE TO LIVE OUT THIS CODE BETTER?

MORE NOTES

MORE NOTES

MORE NOTES

MORE NOTES

MORE NOTES

MORE NOTES

MORE NOTES

Eight Codes of Conduct and Values for Dangerous Women

CODE i: She Takes Her Rightful Place.

CODE ii: She Walks In Her Identity, Inheritance and Value.

CODE iii: She Understands the Difference Between Who She Is and What She Does.

CODE iv: She Lives Out Her Powerful Influence.

CODE v: She Understands How Her Words and Actions Represent Herself.

CODE vi: She Takes Risks.

CODE vii: She Doesn't Look For the Lazy or Easy Way, Nor Does She Make Excuses.

CODE viii: She Values Character & Reputation Over Status Quo.

Made in the USA
Las Vegas, NV
06 October 2023